A GIFT OF
PUDDINGS

A GIFT OF
PUDDINGS

Margot Coatts
Drawings by Ian Beck

BELLEW PUBLISHING
London

For Patrick O'Connor, in New York

First published in Great Britain in 1988 by
Bellew Publishing Company Limited
7 Southampton Place, London WC1A 2DR

British Library Cataloguing in Publication Data
Coatts, Margot
A gift of puddings.
1. Food : Christmas dishes – Recipes
I. Title
641.5'66

ISBN 0 947792 09 0

Printed and bound in Italy by New Interlitho, Milan

CONTENTS

A dozen friends have helped with this short book, prepared in an even shorter amount of time. Warm thanks are especially due to Susan Bosence, Jane Brickell, Lizzie Holmes, Judith Howard, Julia King, Roderick Thorne and Judy Walker, who edited the manuscript. Michael Launchbury checked ingredients against methods and added up quantities; any errors, however, remain my own.

Margot Coatts

INTRODUCTION

This collection of puddings has been conceived as a gift, both to cooks and their friends and families. Many of the recipes are candidates for all-year-round menus, and some are especially good at Christmas.

The book's six acts are designed to help cooks create a culinary programme for Christmas or for any busy period when entertaining is uppermost. The recipes walk the tightrope between the traditional Christmas fare of serious puddings and mince pies, and the more modern feast which might include lightweight ices and sweets of a late twentieth-century disposition. Simple and unselfconscious dishes rub shoulders with the fiddly and the staged. The host may match them to prevailing circumstances or personal preferences, to town or country.

Certain foods have become associated with the Christmas spread. Oranges and mandarins appear here in fritters, flavouring for a pudding mix, as a hot sauce and, yet again, in pancakes. Raspberries, frequently used as a foil to conventional Christmas dishes, are cast as ice cream or whim wham (trifle). Nuts (who can remember a Christmas without them?) perform well either glazed or iced, and make several appearances in fruit puddings and the chocolate log, where they are employed simply to vary the texture.

Alcohol can be a rewarding adjunct to cooking, and who is to notice how little is left in the bottle after the recipe is completed? At least half-a-dozen kinds of drinks are given walk-on parts in these recipes, but this need not prove expensive if miniatures are used. Brandy is the one indispensable spirit. It is the source of the *flambé* effect, beloved of all plum pudding image-makers, and doubles as a preservative and flavourer in the kitchen. Sherry, composed partly of brandy, can frequently be used as its understudy, and is a good all-rounder in savoury cooking, too; it blends particularly well with mushrooms and with pork.

The store cupboard takes on a more sustaining image as the days grow frosty. As well as the usual dried fruits, shelled nuts, glacé cherries and mixed peel – all required for the rich fruit puddings and mincemeats of winter – it is useful to have dried apricots, mangoes and rare fruits. Generous supplies of eggs, flour, spices and essences will give greater range to the culinary repertoire, leaving only fruits, greenery and dairy products to be purchased at the last minute. In the freezer, have fruit purées, syrups and concentrated juices ready to play their parts.

A word of advice on settings and backstage facilities. Nothing is worse than a cramped dressing room, so if your larder is too small clear a space in utility room, cellar or tool shed, where both stores and cooked food can be kept cool until their cues are called. Camouflage and cover your creations lest mice or, worse, children devour them. On the first night, present them on fitting dishes, with informal garnishes, sympathetic lighting and a suitable soundtrack, and pray that the offerings are well-received.

Margot Coatts
July 1988

CLASSIC CHRISTMAS
PUDDINGS

Everyone recognises a Christmas pudding: it is huge, dark brown, heavy, sweet and sticky. The *Rich Plum Pudding* included here is all of these, and highly spiced; a little of everything in the pantry goes in. Like a good stew, the longer it cooks, the better it tastes, and during cooking, it miraculously binds itself together and deepens in colour. The initial boiling is the key to it all – steady and constant. Afterwards, a plum pudding can be stored for months. On Christmas Day, restore it to its steaming glory by re-boiling for two hours or so. On Boxing Day, eat it cold, sliced and spread with brandy butter, or try it fried for breakfast.

A recipe which offers the flavour of Christmas pudding without the heat, weight and work is *Stout Pudding Ice*. It is biscuit-coloured, strong and chewy. All good puds take a couple of days of watchful preparation, and this one is no exception. An extended soaking period is necessary for the fruit; this takes the place of the long boil of a cooked pudding. The ice is quickly completed by the addition of nuts, whipped cream and egg whites; it keeps well in the freezer, and its coolness is a bonus to the busy Christmas cook.

For a more unconventional hot pudding, you can make *Oxenham Pudding à la Noel*, employing a battery of dried fruit but eliminating the usual trio of prunes, mixed peel and suet. Dates, apricots and bananas appear instead, giving an exotic and a much purer pudding. The version here is a hand-me-down from Oxenham Farm in Devon. It is free from added sugar and highly suitable for the health-conscious.

STOUT PUDDING ICE

3 oz pitted prunes (85 g)
1 oz dried apricots (28 g)
1 oz glacé cherries (28 g)
1 oz sultanas (28 g)
1 oz candied peel (28 g)
1 oz muscat raisins (28 g)
1 teaspoon allspice
1 teaspoon cinnamon
4 tablespoons stout

1 tablespoon fresh orange juice
2 tablespoons castor sugar
1 oz ground almonds (28 g)
1 oz blanched almonds (28 g)
2 oz walnut pieces (55 g)
5 fl. oz double cream (140 ml)
5 fl. oz single cream (140 ml)
5 fl. oz natural yoghurt (140 ml)
2 egg whites, whipped

Put all the fruits and spices into a mixing bowl, pour over the stout and orange juice, add 1 tablespoon castor sugar and soak for at least 12 hours (preferably for 24). Stir from time to time, making sure that the apricots are well immersed in the liquor. When the fruit is suitably swollen, strain off the liquor and set aside. Roughly chop the larger fruit and break up the nuts, if necessary; if you prefer a finer mix, a food processor will make short work of this operation. Amalgamate the fruit, nuts and ground almonds. Whisk the double cream, gradually adding the single cream, the yoghurt and the liquor. In a separate bowl, whisk the egg whites until they stand in peaks and add the remaining sugar, as for meringues. Mix the cream into the fruit and nuts; last of all, fold in the egg whites. Press into a chilled and oiled 2-pint mould or basin, and cover with thick cooking foil. Freeze for 6 hours.

When you are ready to serve the ice, dip the mould in hot water, up to the rim. Loosen the edges and allow the outside of the ice to melt a little. Place a glass plate over the pudding, invert and turn out with a shake. Garnish the dish with glazed nuts (*see* page 44).

This recipe weighs about 1½ lb (0.70 kg) and serves 8 people comfortably.

RICH PLUM PUDDING

5 oz chopped suet (140 g)
4 oz breadcrumbs (brown and white) (110 g)
1½ oz cornflour (40 g)
1 oz ground almonds (28 g)
6 oz raisins (170 g)
4 oz sultanas (110 g)
6 oz pitted prunes (chopped) (170 g)
3 oz currants (85 g)
5 oz dark brown sugar (140 g)
2 oz mixed peel (55 g)

1 teaspoon allspice
1 teaspoon nutmeg
1 teaspoon cinnamon
1 teaspoon baking powder
pinch of salt

2 tablespoons lemon juice
3 medium eggs, beaten
1 tablespoon brandy
5 fl. oz sherry, medium (140 ml)

Mix all the dry ingredients in a very large bowl or basin, using clean hands instead of a spoon. Work all the fruit into the mix, taking care to coat all the sticky particles and separate them. Bind all together with the lemon juice, beaten eggs, the brandy and sherry. (Strong ale can be substituted for the latter if preferred, or sherry and brandy may be used in equal proportions.) Leave the mixture to soak for 1 hour at least, then pack very firmly into a buttered 2½-pint basin or plain old china mould. Cover and boil for 5 hours on a low heat.

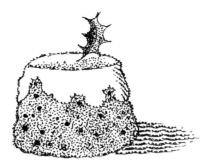

Boiling: This useful modern method eliminates the need for a pudding cloth or string. First, place a 10-inch (25-cm) square of buttered foil over the basin, cover with an upsidedown heatproof saucer or tea plate, press well down and finish by firmly wrapping the foil down the sides of the basin. During boiling, water will collect in the gulley around the saucer and may be spooned away; it cannot harm the pudding. For further protection, invert a foil or metal tart plate over the whole, like an umbrella. The basin itself should rest on a trivet, and stand up to its rim in water inside a large lidded pan. During boiling, secure the lid with a weight or use a teatowel twisted or knotted over the lid and round the handles. Check the water level every hour or so.

At the end of 5 hours, turn off the heat and let the pudding cool overnight. Remove the foil and cover the pudding's surface with a circle of greaseproof paper, moistened with brandy. Tie down with a clean white cloth (an old table napkin is useful) and store in a cool airy place for up to 6 months.

To reheat, steam the pudding gently for 2 hours, using the 'umbrella' method mentioned above. Let it rest for a few minutes before turning out. Serve with flaming brandy and a warm wine custard sauce (*see* page 42). A rich pudding will not need anything more.

The pudding weighs about 3 lb (1.35 kg) and serve 8 to 10.

OXENHAM PUDDING A LA NOEL

6 oz dried wild apricots or peaches (170 g)
3 oz sun-dried dates (85 g)
3 oz seeded muscat raisins (85 g)
4 oz sultanas (110 g)
2 oz dried bananas, unsweetened (55 g)
2 oz glacé cherries, uncoloured (55 g)
2 oz chopped walnuts (55 g)
2 oz unsalted cashews (55 g)
2 oz nibbed almonds (55 g)
3 oz ground almonds (85 g)

½ teaspoon cinnamon
1 teaspoon baking powder
2 teaspoons desiccated coconut
small pinch of salt

1 tablespoon orange flower water
2 tablespoons whisky
4 tablespoons fresh mandarin juice
zest of 1 mandarin or orange
2 large egg yolks, beaten

Mix all the ingredients, except the eggs, in a large bowl. Cover and leave to stand in a cool place for at least 2 days, stirring occasionally. Take approximately half the mixture and chop in a food processor, leaving the other half intact. Beat the eggs and stir them into the amalgam, adding more mandarin juice if it seems too dry. Pack the pudding into a buttered 2-pint basin or mould, cover and boil for 5 hours using the method described in *Rich Plum Pudding* on page 13.

During boiling, this light-coloured and purist pudding miraculously turns dark and aromatic. It needs only a bare hour to reheat and can be served at any season with a garnish of green leaves and a bowl of whipped cream dusted with freshly grated nutmeg.

The pudding weighs about 2 lb (0.90 kg), serves 8 and keeps for a month.

STOCKING FILLERS

Filling Christmas stockings, or stomachs, demands bulk combined with imagination. The traditional way of filling stocking toes and heels has always been to push in the odd piece of fruit. The same applies to these recipes.

Yellow Peach Loaf is a sophisticated and rich cake which contains coconut to open the texture and peach to moisten it. The loaf is perfectly at home served hot at a dinner party, where its blistered surface might cause comment, but is equally suited to being wrapped up and transported on picnics. Out of doors, it can be served 'undressed', without a sauce, from a paper napkin.

By contrast, *Tropical Cobbler* is a filling, old-fashioned dish, consisting simply of fruit with a scone topping. For this book, however, it has been transformed by the use of a variety of exotic fruits (now available dried at any time of year) made into a compote with rhubarb. If rhubarb is out of season when you come to try this dish, substitute tinned fruit and reduce the fluids accordingly.

Pears are available nearly all the year round, but for *Pantomime Pears*, they must be really rock hard. The best way to cook this dish is overnight in an Aga, but if that proves impossible to arrange, turn your oven down to the lowest setting and cook the pears for the length of time it takes to visit the pantomime or theatre. The pudding will be ready on your return.

TROPICAL COBBLER

1 lb fresh rhubarb (450 g)
4 fl. oz thick orange juice (110 ml)
2 fl. oz rum (55 ml)
4 oz dried pears (110 g)
4 oz dried pineapple wedges (110 g)
3 oz dried papaya (85 g)
3 oz dried mangoes (85 g)
4 oz fresh banana (110 g)
2 fl. oz mineral water (55 ml)
pinch of salt

1 dessertspoon lime juice concentrate
12 oz self-raising flour (340 g)
1 teaspoon salt
4 oz salted butter (110 g)
2 oz castor sugar (55 g)
6 fl. oz full-cream milk (170 ml)

For brushing over
½ oz butter (melted) (14 g)
1 tablespoon milk

Trim and rinse the rhubarb, and cut into 2-inch (5-cm) sticks. Place in a heavy-lidded pan with the orange juice, lime juice and rum, cover and poach for 10 minutes; do not sweeten. Leave the now-mushy fruit in the warm juices and add the dried pears, pineapple, papaya and mangoes. If these have been bought whole, cut them into pieces approximately 2 inches (5 cm) long and ½ inch (1.2 cm) wide. Leave the compote for 24 hours to soak and swell; add only a *tiny* pinch of salt and no other seasonings. Chop the banana and stir in. Transfer the fruit to a shallow baking dish, cover with cooking foil and bake for about 45 minutes at gas no. 5 (375°F/190°C).

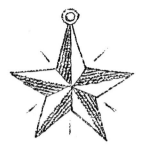

Meanwhile, make the cobbler or scone topping. Place the flour, salt and cubed, cold butter in a food processor and run it for 10 seconds, until the mixture resembles breadcrumbs. Add the sugar, mix again, then gradually pour in the milk with the machine still running. Stop the moment a dough is formed. Flour a large board and press out the dough, turning it frequently; make a slab about ¾ inch (2 cm) thick to fit the baking dish containing the fruit. Lay the topping over this, trim off any excess, smooth the curves by hand and liberally brush some melted butter and milk over the surface. Place on a baking sheet in the oven and cook at gas no. 7 (425°F/220°C) for 15 minutes or until golden and well-risen. Eat hot with *crème fraîche* or clotted cream.

These quantities make two 5-person dishes or one giant 10-person one.

PANTOMIME PEARS

6 large, hard Conference pears
1 tumbler red wine
½ tumbler mineral water
3 tablespoons white sugar

1 teaspoon cinnamon
20–30 Brazil nuts
1 dessertspoon redcurrant jelly
sprig of lemon balm (if available)

Very carefully peel the pears, retaining the stalk and flower remains at the base of the fruit. Stand them upright, closely packed, in a lidded casserole, preferably one with an air hole. Mix up the wine, water, sugar and cinnamon in a jug and pour over the pears; it should cover them to at least half their height. Poach at gas no. 1 (275°F/140°C) for at least 5 hours, turning or re-arranging the fruit once so that it is stained red all over. Drop in the nuts at this point, which may be any time up to half an hour before serving.

When the pears are cooked to perfection, keep them warm. Ladle off the liquor into a small pan and boil it rapidly until a syrup is formed. Add the redcurrant jelly and a sprig of lemon balm (if in season) for extra flavour. Set the pears and a few nuts on individual plates and pour over the hot syrup so that it forms both a glaze and a sauce. Eat with soft-whipped cream.

Allow 1 large or two small pears per person; increase the liquids and sugar according to the size of the baking dish in use.

18

YELLOW PEACH LOAF

6 oz butter (170 g) or 4 oz cooking butter (110 g)
8 oz white sugar (225 g)
2 large egg yolks
8 oz self-raising flour (225 g)
2 oz desiccated coconut (55 g)
4 tablespoons milk
pinch of salt
large peach or tinned equivalent (about 4 oz/110 g)

Pouring sauce
6 oz castor sugar (170 g)
2 oz butter (55 g)
6 tablespoons milk
1 dessertspoon apricot brandy (optional)

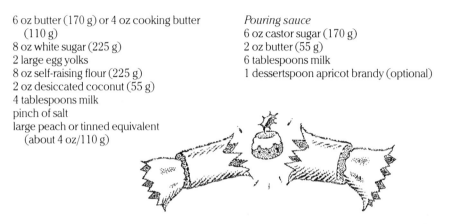

Using a food processor or electric mixer (or by hand), cream the butter and sugar together until light and fluffy, then gradually add the egg yolks. Slowly add the flour, coconut, milk and salt. Stop mixing as soon as the flour is amalgamated; the mixture will be reasonably sloppy. Butter a loaf tin measuring approximately 9 × 5 × 2½ inches (23 × 13 × 6 cm) and fill with the mixture. Slice the peach very finely and arrange it on top (it will soon sink in); pour over any juice saved from the peach. Bake at gas no. 3 (325°F/170°C) for 1 hour, or until a skewer inserted into the centre comes out clean.

Turn the cake out into a shallow baking dish. The surface should be sticky and soft; brown it by toasting under the grill set at a low heat. Meanwhile, make up a thin, hot sauce by mixing together the sugar, butter and milk with the brandy (if you have it); boil to reduce slightly. Slice the loaf at the table; place each piece on a warm, medium-sized grey or blue plate and pour a pool of sauce beside it.

The loaf serves 8 and is very popular with children (for them, omit the apricot brandy).

CHRISTMAS CRACKERS

The crackers are recipes to surprise and excite. The *Lime and Cucumber Jelly* is a very good-looking, transparent palate cleanser. It may be eaten as a starter, between courses or as a sweet. If you eat cream with your jelly (a barbaric habit), only soured will do.

Wiltshire Chocolate Log is a squelchy pud. At first glance, the recipe seems a complicated one, but is in fact two distinct short jobs plus one deft combining action. Be prepared for a lot of whisking; an electric hand-held machine gives the most sensitive but fast treatment. The classic *roulade* comes, of course, from France, but this one travelled via Wiltshire, accumulating modifications along the way.

The idea for *Chinese Lanterns* is the attraction of opposites: hot with cold, sharp with smooth, crisp with wobbly. This is toy food, for fun, and should be treated as such. The colours, cream and orange, can be enhanced by setting the strange concoction on a lurid art deco dish, pouring the sauce over and setting light to it.

CHINESE LANTERNS

Creams
¼ oz leaf gelatine (7 g)
½ pint milk (280 ml)
¼ pint whipping cream (140 ml)
2 oz stem ginger (55 g)
3 dessertspoons stem ginger syrup

Fritters
pinch of salt
4 oz plain flour (110 g)
1 medium egg
¼ pint full cream-milk (140 ml)
12 oz mandarin segments (340 g)
   (or fruit pieces)

Cut up the leaf gelatine by snipping with kitchen scissors, and put the pieces in a small pan with 4 tablespoons of milk to cover. Warm gently over a low heat, stirring frequently, until it has dissolved. Meanwhile whip the cream and chop the ginger into very tiny chips. Add the ginger and its syrup to the cream and whisk in the liquified gelatine. Pour the ginger cream into wetted individual moulds or small coffee cups to set. Place in the coldest part of the fridge for at least 3 hours. When you are ready to cook the fritters, first dip the moulds or cups in a basin of very hot water to loosen the creams, and turn each cream out on to a medium-sized plate.

To make the fritters, first de-seed the mandarin segments and dry them on paper towel. Make the batter in a liquidiser, preferably an hour or two in advance. Put the flour and salt into the goblet and run the machine for a few seconds; add the egg and milk and mix until a thick smooth batter is obtained. Transfer the batter to a basin. The fritters can be shallow or deep fried; heat light oil, or oil and lard. (Test the heat by dropping in a teaspoon of batter; it should rise immediately to the surface, sizzling.) Holding the mandarin segments with tongs or skewers, coat them in batter and drop them into the hot fat and remove them when crisp. Serve 6 or 8 hot fritters beside each ginger cream, with an orange sauce *flambé* if desired (*see* page 42).

This recipe makes 4 coffee-cup-sized creams plus an accompanying cluster of fritters.

WILTSHIRE CHOCOLATE LOG

4 large, or 5 small, eggs (separated)
6 oz castor sugar (170 g)
6 oz best plain chocolate (170 g)
4 teaspoons whisky
1 teaspoon instant coffee powder
1 oz cooking butter (28 g)
icing sugar or *sucre de vanille*
2 oz nibbed almonds (55 g)

Crème patissière filling
2 yolks, 1 white of egg
2 oz castor sugar (55 g)
1 oz cornflour (28 g)
1 oz plain flour (28 g)
½ pint milk (280 ml)
vanilla essence to taste

Beat the egg whites in a large bowl until stiff, then set aside. Whisk the yolks with the sugar until creamy-looking. Break up the chocolate and melt it in a small pan with the whisky, coffee powder and butter; allow to cool a little, then pour in the yolks and sugar, mixing in the saucepan. Fold all this into the egg whites, adding the nibbed almonds. Line a Swiss roll or other shallow cake tin (approximately 8 × 13 × 1 inches/20 × 33 × 2.5 cm) with buttered greaseproof paper. Tip in the mixture, and shake to level. Bake for 15–20 minutes in a moderate oven, gas no. 4 or 5 (350–375°F/180–190°C).

Tip out the cake on to a sheet of greaseproof paper covered in sieved icing sugar or *sucre de vanille*. While the cake cools, make the *crème patissière*. Break the yolks into a bowl, add 1 oz (28 g) of sugar, and cream well with a handwhisk or fork. Add both flour and cornflour, sieved, and about a quarter of the milk. Heat the rest of the milk to boiling point and pour it into the yolks, stirring continuously; blend well and return to the boil. After it has thickened, remove the mixture from the heat and turn it into a basin to cool. Whisk one egg white with the remaining sugar until it stands in peaks, then whisk the cooling *crème* and carefully incorporate it into the egg white. Finally, add a few drops of vanilla essence.

Spread the cool chocolate cake with the warm *crème* and gently roll it up, using the paper as a base. The *roulade* will inevitably split and crack in the rolling, but this only enhances its log-like appearance, especially when dusted with icing sugar or *sucre de vanille*. The log may be decorated with almond paste animals and birds, as described on page 43.

The log will easily serve 8.

LIME AND CUCUMBER JELLY

1 oz leaf gelatine (28 g)
½ pint tonic water (280 ml)
4 tablespoons lime juice cordial
4 tablespoons pale cream sherry

castor sugar to taste
½ cucumber
½ lime
mint sprigs

Break up the leaf gelatine and put it in a milk pan with the tonic water. Warm over a very low heat for about 20 minutes, or until the gelatine has dissolved completely; do not allow it to boil. Remove any scum and transfer the gelatine to a measuring jug; add the lime cordial, sherry and additional tonic water, as necessary, up to the 1-pint (570-ml) mark. Stir vigorously. Remove any further froth by dragging a piece of paper towel over the surface of the liquid. Test for sweetness and add castor sugar if desired; remember, warm jelly tastes rather unpleasant!

Slice finely about 1½ inches (3.5 cm) of cucumber, and snip into quarter circles with kitchen scissors. Strip the smallest leaves from the mint. Pour the jelly mixture into individual glasses, drop cucumber segments and a mint sprig into each, and chill for 3 hours. Top with chopped cucumber and lime slices to serve.

Makes 8 small glasses.

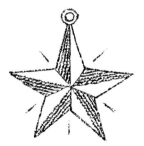

QUICK CHRISTMAS

Pancakes make a special breakfast, brunch or pudding course. They keep well for a few days in the fridge (rolled, folded in four or simply laid flat on sheets of greaseproof paper) and they can be re-heated satisfactorily in a steamer, wrapped in foil. Some people like their pancakes stuffed, but surely the best accompaniments are sugar and citrus juice. Pour the batter sparingly into the pan to make *Mean Marmalade Pancakes* and just *show* them a segment of orange or lemon.

Sixth-Sense Syllabub and *Whim Wham* (an eighteenth-century term for trifle) are the puddings to make when you are short of time and in need of an alcoholic reviver. Both look impressive and taste pleasantly aromatic; even the diet-conscious will try a mouthful and finish their helping. Don't stint on the cream and buy the very best available: untreated and unpackaged is infinitely superior to the famous brand names.

PS Try figs instead of raspberries in the Whim Wham. Irresistible.

27

MEAN MARMALADE PANCAKES

4 oz plain flour (110 g)
pinch of salt
2 medium eggs
½ pint full-cream milk (280 ml)
2 level dessertspoons castor sugar

3 level dessertspoons marmalade
1 oz butter or lard (28 g)
2 oranges or lemons
(according to flavour of marmalade)

Put the flour and salt in a liquidiser goblet and run the machine for a few seconds to aerate the flour. Break the eggs into the flour, then add the milk sparingly, with the machine running. Spoon in the sugar and marmalade and mix thoroughly. (Alternatively, you can mix together the flour and salt by hand; add the eggs and blend; then mix in the milk gradually; finish by adding the sugar and marmalade.) Cover the batter and leave it to stand for at least 1 hour, but preferably overnight.

To cook, melt the butter or lard in an omelette pan, but only enough to just cover the surface and make it glisten and smoke very slightly; remove any surplus fat. Pour in enough mixture to cover the pan 'meanly' and fry the pancake over a slow, steady heat until it is light brown underneath. Turn it, transfer it on to a plate and sprinkle with castor sugar and, if you wish, pass it quickly under the grill. Squeeze orange or lemon juice over and eat.

Makes 8 6-inch (15-cm) pancakes.

SIXTH-SENSE SYLLABUB

8 fl. oz double cream (230 ml)
3 fl. oz medium dry white wine (85 ml)
1 dessertspoon Armagnac or brandy

1 dessertspoon castor sugar
1 teaspoon fresh lemon juice
20–25 white grapes

This syllabub, made with dry white wine and sugar, may not be quite authentic, but by taking up some of the liquids, the sugar improves the bulk and hence the long life of the pudding. It does, however, separate in time. To colour the syllabub a creamy yellow, use either Jersey cream or a deep-toned wine.

Whip the cream until it starts to stiffen, then gradually whisk in three-quarters of the wine, the Armagnac or brandy, the sugar and, lastly, the lemon juice. De-pip and chop up the grapes on a saucer, to catch the juice. Add the grapes to the cream mixture, whisking lightly, and pour in the remaining wine and grape juice at the last twirl of the whisk; it should almost leave a trail through the syllabub.

Spoon into chilled glasses or custard cups, wind a strand of vine leaves around the glasses and eat the syllabub within an hour of making.

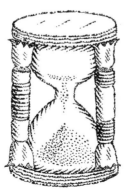

WHIM WHAM

Quantities are per person, using custard glasses:
1 thin slice ginger cake
1 oz frozen raspberries (28 g)
1 dessertspoon kirsch
1 dessertspoon raspberry juice or bottled syrup

Topping
2 thin ginger biscuits
1 dessertspoon vanilla ice cream or
   thick Greek yoghurt
1 dessertspoon pouring cream
5 whole toasted almonds

If you are making this dish in winter, defrost the raspberries; fresh raspberries are, of course, much better.

First, cut the ginger cake into cubes. Half fill each glass with cake and pour over the kirsch and the raspberry syrup. (The tinned or bottled French syrups are best.) Meanwhile, toast or fry some whole almonds in butter, dry them on paper towel and leave to cool.

Fill the remainder of each glass with raspberries and top up with ice cream or yoghurt; add a spoonful of cream and the toasted almonds. Delicate ginger biscuits may be offered round to eat with the Whim Wham.

EMERGENCY RATIONS

Christmas and holiday times always bring unexpected guests, and you will use all your energy keeping them amused with conversation and games – plus a constant supply of food and drink. These three Emergency Rations are designed as keepable teatime or late night snacks to supplement the main fare.

The *Bakewell Pudding*, from the celebrated Derbyshire town, will satisfy the most hungry outdoor type, while the delicate *Victorian Rice Cake* could happily grace a nineteenth-century tea party.

Nowadays, a homemade mincemeat shows a real devotion to kitchen craft; the one included here originated in the 1940s at a Suffolk farmhouse where, one imagines, the oven was never cold. Three ways are suggested for using *Apricot Mincemeat* as two-bite snacks; it is also excellent as a stuffing for baked apples or family-sized turnovers.

APRICOT MINCEMEAT

8 oz apricots (225 g)
4 oz dates (110 g)
2 oz raisins (55 g)
2 oz sultanas (55 g)
2 oz sweet apple (55 g)
2 oz shredded suet (55 g)
4 oz brown sugar (110 g)

1 oz chopped almonds (28 g)
¼ oz ground nutmeg (7 g)
1 lime
1 tablespoon whisky or brandy

To decorate
angelica strips

Mince the apricots and the dates and leave them to soak overnight in 1 tablespoon of whisky or brandy and 3 or 4 tablespoons of water. Next day, peel, core and finely chop the apples and mix them with all the dry ingredients; add the apricots and dates, draining off any surplus liquid. Pare the rind from the lime, slice it, and stir it into the mincemeat with about 1 tablespoon of the juice. Pack the mincemeat into an earthenware crock, cover with greaseproof paper dipped in brandy, and seal; keep cool. This makes about 1½ lb (0.70 kg), and is ready to eat after 1 week and preferably within 1 month.

This quantity of mincemeat will make about 2 dozen conventional mince pies or a much larger number of miniature ones. These look particularly good made in *petits fours* cases or tiny patty pans; instead of pastry lids, cover them with a thin layer of white glacé icing (*see* page 44), and put a sprig of angelica on top. Another variant, sometimes known as *Santa's Perks*, are mincemeat *croustades*. The casings are made from thin slices of white bread which have been buttered both sides, trimmed with scissors, pressed into steep-sided individual pie tins and baked in a very hot oven for about 5 minutes. Fill the casings with mincemeat, make tops (using the same technique) and return the *croustades* to a medium oven for a further 5 minutes.

BAKEWELL PUDDING

8 oz puff pastry (225 g)
1 tablespoon milk
4 oz plum or raspberry jam (110 g)
1½ oz unsalted butter (45 g)
1½ oz castor sugar (45 g)

1 egg
2 oz self-raising flour (55g)
2 oz freshly ground almonds (55 g)
glacé icing (optional)

Line a 9- or 10-inch (25-cm) pie plate with puff pastry; turn the edges back on themselves to form a thick, cushion-like rim, about 1 inch (2.5 cm) wide. Brush with milk. Spread the uncooked pastry base thickly with jam. To make the sponge topping, cream the butter and sugar together; then add the egg, flour and ground almonds. (The strongest almond flavour is obtained by grinding the nuts yourself, just prior to use.) Bake for 30 minutes at gas no. 4 (350°F/180°C) and ice when cold (*see* page 44). The pudding keeps well in a tin and is best served warm, with or without cream.

This pudding serves 6 hikers or 8 chess-players.

VICTORIAN RICE CAKE

8 oz best-quality plain rice (225 g)
2 medium eggs
5 fl. oz single cream (140 ml)
3 oz castor sugar (85 g)
½ teaspoon vanilla or almond essence

zest of 1 lemon
nutmeg
1 oz butter (28 g)
small pinch of salt

Wash the rice well, changing the water 6 times. Boil until just tender, using 2 cups of water to each cup of wet rice. Drain and cool in a large colander. Beat the eggs and cream together in a large bowl and add the castor sugar, essence, zest of lemon and salt. (Experiment with coloured syrups, omitting the sugar, for children.) Add the rice to the flavoured eggs, cream and sugar and leave the mixture to stand for 10 minutes. Meanwhile, generously butter a heart-shaped cake tin or individual patty pans. Adjust the flavouring and moisture content with essence and cream, and mix in plenty of freshly-grated nutmeg; if it is the right consistency, the mixture should stir easily, like a thick soup. Pour the rice into the tin(s) and dot with slivers of butter. Bake at gas no. 5 (375°F/190°C) for 25–30 minutes. Turn out when completely cold. Dredge with castor sugar, or chocolate dust (put a 'flake' in the grinder).

This serves up to 10.

ICE PACKS

This section is devised to appeal to all tastes. *Arcadian Ice Cream* is for the health-conscious cook who believes, correctly, that the food of the gods – nuts, raisins and honey – will keep the body's machinery running smoothly.

For junk-food lovers, children especially, whisked evaporated milk combines with fruit and bread (yes, bread) in a recipe of such banality that all readers will want to stock up with *Rough Raspberry Ice Cream*.

Sorbets can be made of anything watery, but they usually look so *tasteful*. *Blue Curaçao Sorbet* is different: pale blue and faintly medicinal. The host offering this one will certainly be skating on thin ice.

37

ARCADIAN ICE CREAM

½ teacup desiccated coconut
½ teacup fat raisins
   (muscat or similar)
½ teacup unsalted cashew nuts
1 tablespoon clear honey
2 drops vanilla essence

2½ fl. oz single cream (70 ml)
5 fl. oz double cream (140 ml)
1 large egg white
grated nutmeg (garnish)

This is a quick ice cream to make in which everything is simply measured in teacups. (A full teacup holds a quarter of a pint.) First, coat the raisins and nuts in honey and set aside. Beat the double cream until light and fluffy. In a separate bowl, beat the egg white, mix in the vanilla essence and single cream; then amalgamate all the ingredients. Lastly, swirl in the fruit and nut mixture, using a knife. Freeze in a container about 1½ inches (3.5 cm) deep, with a cover. After 2 hours, remove from the freezer, whisk and re-freeze. Spoon into glass dishes and dust with freshly grated nutmeg. (The mixture performs particularly well if the egg and cream are chilled in advance.)

This recipe serves 8, and is best eaten within one month.

ROUGH RASPBERRY ICE CREAM

7 oz can evaporated milk (200 g)
2 oz icing sugar (55 g)

2 oz white breadcrumbs (55 g)
6 oz frozen raspberry purée (170 g)

Make the ice in a medium-sized bowl – preferably one of toughened glass – which will be used to freeze and serve it. Whisk the evaporated milk until thick and frothy, then slowly whisk in the icing sugar. Grind the breadcrumbs and liquidise the fruit (a fruit and syrup mix may be used), adding a little water if necessary. Sieve the fruit purée and fold it with the breadcrumbs into the whisked milk; test for sweetness. Cover and freeze. Beat the mixture twice, at hourly intervals; cover, seal and freeze. The ice cream should be removed to the main part of the fridge an hour before serving.

This serves 4 or 5, and keeps well for up to 2 months.

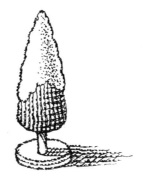

BLUE CURAÇAO SORBET

4 oz sugar (110 g)
½ pint water (280 ml)
4 oz kiwi fruit (110 g)
2 dessertspoons blue curaçao

2 large, or 3 small, egg whites
granulated sugar and candied flowers
or mint leaves to garnish

Put the sugar and water into a heavy pan and bring them to the boil; stir until all the sugar has dissolved and the mixture has turned into a thin syrup. Cool. Peel and chop the kiwi fruit; put them into a liquidiser with the blue curaçao to make a purée. Strain the purée into the syrup and pour the mixture (by now a bright jade green) into a glass or metal mixing bowl. Refrigerate to chill completely. Meanwhile, whisk the egg whites until they stand in peaks; fold into the kiwi and blue curaçao mixture. Freeze for 2 hours, or until the sorbet is semi-set. Re-whisk in the same bowl, cover closely and re-freeze for 6 hours.

Serve with a little sugar sprinkled on top and some candied flowers or mint leaves to decorate (*see* page 47). The sorbet looks particularly good when piled high on a transparent glass stand.

PARTY TRICKS

WINE CUSTARD

(for puddings and pies)

½ pint sweet white wine (280 ml)
2 egg yolks

2 tablespoons pouring cream

Boil the wine in a small pan to reduce it by half. Break the egg yolks into a basin and beat in the cream; then slowly pour in the hot wine, whisking continuously. Strain the mixture back into the pan, sweeten if you must, and warm over a low heat, stirring, until a custard is formed which will coat the back of a spoon. Serve warm from a small tureen.

ORANGE SAUCE FLAMBE

(for *Chinese Lanterns*)

4 tablespoons orange juice

6 tablespoons brandy

Boil the orange juice in a small heavy pan to reduce it slightly. (If you use orange juice concentrate instead, take two tablespoons straight from the bottle.) Add the brandy and warm the mixture briefly. Pour the sauce over the ginger creams, drop some fritters beside them on the plates, and set light to the sauce.

ALMOND PASTE ANIMALS
BIRDS AND ACORNS
(for *Wiltshire Chocolate Log*)

Paste
½ lb icing sugar (225 g)
1 large egg white
4 oz ground almonds (110 g)
1 dessertspoon brandy or sherry

Extras
edible food colouring
egg white
almond flakes or splits
walnut halves
4 oz milk chocolate (melted) (110 g)
ground cinnamon or powdered cocoa

Sieve the icing sugar; lightly whisk the egg white. Put all the ingredients for the paste into a heavy mixing bowl and knead to a dough. This will produce a very smooth, pale paste, suitable for modelling. If a more 'crunchy' one is required, substitute castor for icing sugar. (Reserve half of the mixture for the stuffed dates on p. 46.)

Animals, birds and acorns are best made 2 days in advance. Follow the drawings below for general shapes: make the animals 'solid'; for leaves, colour a small amount of paste and roll out to under ¼-inch (5 mm) thick 'sheet'. Stick the various components together with egg white. Use almond flakes to make ears, beaks, and so on, and walnuts for the wings of birds. To produce shading, paint or dip the backs of animals, birds and acorns in melted chocolate or dust with ground cinnamon or powdered cocoa. They will keep well in a tin for a month or so.

GLAZED NUTS

(for various dishes)

1 dessertspoon gelatine powder
2 dessertspoons water

2 dessertspoons honey
6 oz Brazil nuts (170 g)

Dissolve the gelatine powder in water and warm it in a small pan with the honey. Simmer for 2 or 3 minutes until the glaze begins to gel. Drop the nuts into the glaze, stir, then spoon on to a plate and allow to cool for 1 hour. Use to garnish ices or pancakes.

GLACE ICING

1 tablespoon water
1 teaspoon lemon juice

½ lb icing sugar (225 g)

Put the water and lemon juice into a saucepan. Sieve the icing sugar into this. Warm all the ingredients together over a low heat until the sugar has melted. Cool the icing until you can comfortably put your finger in it. Use to cover tarts and pies.

BRANDY AND RUM BUTTERS

(for cold *Christmas Pudding* or hot *Mince Pies*)

4 oz icing sugar (110 g)　　　　　　　　1 dessertspoon brandy or rum
2 oz butter (55 g)

Sieve the icing sugar. Beat the butter with a wooden spoon until it is soft and fluffy; gradually work in the sugar until it is thoroughly blended. Add the brandy or rum by degrees. Pack into a small pot or ramekin and refrigerate. Serves 4. Make several different types of butter and place them round the table.

FROSTED GRAPES

1 lb seedless grapes (450 g)　　　　　　3 fl. oz water (85 ml)
4 oz granulated sugar (110 g)　　　　　4 oz castor sugar (110 g)

Wash the grapes in bunches and dry them thoroughly. Melt the granulated sugar in the water slowly and bring to the boil; this takes about 5 minutes. When a syrup has formed, keep it hot over a low heat. Using tongs, dip the bunches of grapes into it. Have ready a shallow bowl containing the castor sugar and, after shaking the drips from the grapes, smother them in this. Then put them on a wire rack to dry. Snip the grapes from the stems and arrange them on a dish.

BRISK BONBONS

2 oz bitter chocolate (55 g)
1 oz butter (28 g)
3 oz powdered cocoa (85 g)
4 oz icing sugar (110 g)
1 teaspoon vanilla essence
2 dessertspoons evaporated milk

To coat
3 oz chocolate strands and
desiccated coconut mixed together (85 g)

Break up the chocolate and melt it in a pan with the butter. Remove the pan from the heat and add the cocoa powder, sugar, vanilla essence and, lastly, the evaporated milk: work the mixture well until it is thick and smooth. Take a teaspoonful of the mixture at a time and shape it by hand into a ball about the size of a glass marble. Roll each ball in the chocolate strands and coconut until liberally coated.

STUFFED DATES

1 box of good quality dates

6 oz (170 g) almond paste, made from
the recipe on p. 43

Stone the dates by slitting them along one side. Roll the almond paste out into long sausage-shapes, cut into date-like lengths and then press the paste into the dates. If desired, the almond paste mixture can be divided in two and stained red and green with edible food colouring.

EDIBLE POT POURRI

2 or 3 roses
2 or 3 pinks
sprigs of young mint or lemon balm

Coating paste
1 medium egg white
2 oz icing sugar (55 g)
4 oz castor sugar (110 g)

Equipment
baking trays
baking parchment
artist's brush (sable)

Set aside an afternoon to work when there is a good play on the radio. Have ready petals from fresh blooms and a few edible leaves (mint or lemon balm); wash if necessary and dry on paper towel. Lay the petals on a clean surface. Lightly whisk the egg white and sieve the icing sugar. Mix them together to form a smooth, semi-transparent paste; it should be runny but elastic. To coat, hold each petal carefully and paint both sides, using a medium-sized, soft brush. Lay them on a baking tray which has been lined with parchment and sprinkled with castor sugar; sprinkle the painted petals with more castor sugar. (Keep a packet nearby while working.) Preheat the oven to gas no. 1 (275°F/140°C), usually the lowest setting, put in the tray of painted petals and leaves to dry out. Leave the petals in the oven, with the door ajar, for 2 hours. This can be followed up by a further 24 hours in a warm airing cupboard. Do not return the petals to the relatively damp air of the kitchen, but store them in an airtight tin until needed to dress ices, cakes or jellies, or simply to place them about the house in glass bowls.

Of the various garden flowers which can be used, roses taste the best, particularly the highly-scented ones. Choose newly-opened blooms with petals of an attractively curled shape and in contrasting colours.

47

INDEX